NIGHT BLOOMING

POEMS to Speak at Twilight

Polly Alice McCann

An Imprint of Flying Ketchup Press ®
Kansas City, Missouri

Night Blooming

Appreciative acknowledgments to the publications in which the following poems previously appeared: "prayer garden" "Night Blooming" which appeared in Puss 'N Boötes: Dark Poems. "What You See Here" appeared in "365 Days: a poetry anthology, vol. 4"

Copyright © 2022 by Polly Alice McCann. All rights reserved. Except in the case of brief quotations or reviews, no part of this publication may be reproduced or transmitted in any form or by any means without written permission from the publisher. All inquiries should be addressed to:
Flying Ketchup Press
11608 N. Charlotte Street
Kansas City, MO 64115

Library of Congress Cataloging–Publication Data
McCann, Polly Alice.
Night Blooming: Poems to Speak at Twilight / Polly Alice McCann
Library of Congress Control Number:
ISBN– ISBN: 978-1-970151-33-6

To Emily Dickinson, Gary Beaumier, Huascar Medina, and Natty Zan Powers, my inspiration for these poems & to those that survived and emerged from the pandemic 2019-2021

LETTER FROM THE AUTHOR

Dear Poets,

In January of 2022 I was asked to speak at Swordfish Tom's Speakeasy poetry night in November. All year long, I crafted poems I thought would be good to read aloud in the dark. My inspiration was the night I sat in the garden trying to write a poem for a contest due at midnight. I didn't finish the poem in time. It took me all year to finish it. In the end, however, I was happy with the words that emerged. My hope is to make you feel as if the is growing over the low walls, knocking them over and creating another place altogether; one where growth is possible.

These have been dark times and my attempt was to write poems that pushed through that dark. Maybe like me, you spent some of the last year writing letters to family in case you didn't survive the pandemic. Maybe you lost people or things you loved. My goal in these poems was to forget all that, and focus on one day, one audience, with one group of people listening in the dark together.

Another inspiration was nine months of weekly live radio shows, Ketchupedia Poetry Radio, 100.1 FM KONN Kansas City Radio with my cohost Richard Parilla. I've never learned so much as interviewing poets and sharing their work live on the air. During the Covid shut down, I taught from home for two years, often only seeing black boxes with white letters of student names rather than their faces. Going to the radio station and spending time with poets was often the only face I saw that week. It was a growing time, full of beautiful words.

Poems changed for me, to become something which is meant to travel by air. Like a seed; something that grows among friends. I began to think about air, breath, and you, readers. Thank you for reading and listening to these poems. How generous.

Polly Alice

Table of Contents

Afternoon Poesy

Come to the Night Garden 4
Like Sharks 6
Why are poets always talking 7
about flowers? 7
Left or Right Side of the Peonies 8
Bee 10
How to Be Alone, Honeysuckle 11
Five Red Tears, 13
or I am Not a Gardner 13
Poet-Trees 15
Emily Dickinson is addicted to Facebook 17
Turn, Turn Blackened Catfish 21
Justice is Running 26

Evening Rock

Field Stones 30
unedited prayer garden 31
What you see here 32
You try not to think about the dead 34
The Aldica– 35
Jerusalem Café is gone 41
Easter Again 2021 43
Stones 46
Sometimes You Finally get a Moment 47

Night Blooming

Fattening Moon 51
Skyscrapers 52
Night Blooming Flower 54
The Green Lady 56
Like Lightning 57
Moon White Dress 58
"it's a terrible, terrible world." 59
night garden cantos 63
Gems 67
Poetry Prompt with Polly 69

POLLY ALICE MCCANN

Sun Up Strawberry

Sun up! Strawberry sky
swallow the gray dawn
stem the ache from the clasp
of the front door—the kids
have left for school
so early, so early

Sun up! Strawberry sky
the trees are black lightning
the day light a star

Sun low! Cherry Bomb night
the sun balances above
honey hued horizon
a cherry bomb!

Luscious fruit
juicy fire berry
bubblicious supernova
I'd like to tie the stem
with my tongue

NIGHT BLOOMING

Afternoon Poesy

NIGHT BLOOMING

Come to the Night Garden

This year I've submitted more
than ten poems for publication,
more than seventeen, more than
forty, a few hundred, so
none were accepted.
---
applied for a handful of jobs
several a day, a week's worth,
a month of Sundays,
created fifty-two different pages
of my resume to no effect.
---
been stood up a few times
texted on dating apps
none of them for more than a day—
well, one every day for a year,
one never in a dozen years—
one once a year every decade
---
sent out sixty-six letters
without a reply, or maybe,
it was a hundred and five
filled with butterflies—few came back
or if they arrived
hadn't any words in them

So now I can tell you,
just as I'm standing here,
I know the feeling,
I mean it. Like you,
I know the feeling of

R E J E C T I O N
Yes, rejection.
———
So, come. Because there's
enough wind
from these slammed doors—
to blow us away
There're enough clinks
from these locked bars—

NIGHT BLOOMING

to make ourselves
a rake and shovel

———

We'll dig a garden here
and with all the dashes
every teacher told us not to use
between so many phrases–
I'm going to make a sweet little path

---and you can come too. Come
out here with me in the night garden.
where I'll teach you to

( ) speak fluent night flower
( ) interpret the winks of the moon
( ) have a taste for words that root in the dark

- - - - -- -- -- -- -- -- -- -- -- - - - -

Come to the Night Garden
all you need is here.
Listen to earth buzz,
bend to meet the dusk of twilight's
last cingant kiss,
Steel yourself for the cold crush
of a star's smile
refracting dewdrop style.

Come to the Night Garden
where we can mend together–
divide our sorrows into rows
and wait for new things to grow–
It doesn't matter what we bury here,
bodies or bones, bread, or baskets,
tares or tears,
we have until the wind chimes. Yeah,
we have until chimes.

NIGHT BLOOMING

Like Sharks

Winter trees, like sharks,
cast their night stars,
their night stares, reach
up rosy fingers to the dawn
as I reach for poesy
like the Robin sings for a mate,
reach like the squirrel
for a higher limb, and I
reach for poesy like lightening
for water, reach like the cardinal
to speak in tongues of ghosts
I reach for poesy like snow
that lingers on a cold ground
like my mother for her coffee
like my son for his game
like my daughter to a horizon
of answers in an ocean
of fallen teeth

NIGHT BLOOMING

Why are poets always talking about flowers?

because
poems are flowers
because they start out bud
their terse meanings hidden poems are flowers
because they undertake to disclose a bouquet of rose
unfurling slowly, they revel in their show flowers because
they reveal inside their bitter seed of a word tight behind two lips-
are flowers because they open artless to usher fresh satiating
senses they make known a treasure house of pheromones, colors
we can't see, evince a rare dream, extend arms of truth, evade
wind's harsh blow, and morning's cold, they prove the secrets
of the dark world underneath by baring its light
poems they testify to the truth, they usher in
a sweet clarity, dispelling myths with
displays of power, extend generous
hands of peace, they make
known a better
way

NIGHT BLOOMING

Left or Right Side of the Peonies

Where do you bury your dead?
We moved a thousand miles
to come home to their graves here.
There's the little white Zion church
with headstones that read
Greenberry Poage and *Forest Rose.*

Memorial Day intentions mean
cutting the last peony bloom, and
stragglers of bleeding hearts
to take to the old graves .
Instead, we sleep in
fight away the afternoon until
that paper plate sunset comes quickly.

Who has a map to show the old roads,
so, we won't miss the turn again?

Does it matter that some of my
ancestors expect me–waiting
with earth and soil while others
only looked to sky? Some minded
heaven while others dug deep roots
to the here and now. When everything
was covid closed, Denise brought
something, Great-Great-Grandma Nora's
peonies from an old neighboring farm.

The dirt dry, the cold creeping
close when hope ran short,
we planted them with secret roots
by the maple stump,
and waited through winter's wear.

Until one single white bloom appeared
like a lotus, ancient and wild
golden shafts edged with a breath
of pink in the center
grandma's flower told us
to keep going
keep working

NIGHT BLOOMING

keep cooking dinner
keep mending
and then stop every so often
to wonder

I want to be like her,
the peony that bows between
a beauty, an arc
an unexpected bloom.

NIGHT BLOOMING

Bee

when
i think of a
world
turning
a single day or a single hour
without your song of busy insatiable joy
the sun grows cold
and each flower
shivers
Bee
I

NIGHT BLOOMING

How to Be Alone, Honeysuckle

It was the neighbors from Peru
two girls one tall and plump one small
and skinny, who taught her that every
place on the map has treasure.

How to take the slender blossom
of honeysuckle, remove the stem,
press the stalk in one tender stroke
to produce a bead of pure honey.

How to place the drop on the tongue
just so the flavor explodes.
How to find mulberries
from the trees behind the drive
for making pies. How sweetness
and heat make everything taste better.

Even now as she walks down the path
honeysuckle bushes towering
overhead filling every crevice of sky
inhales their perfume
the pollen making the air

thick as the musk in a small room
where lovers mistakenly
light a candle not knowing that
they'll soon be unable to breathe.

Though she doesn't remember
their names, those girls were the ones
who told her if she tried, she could
teach herself to ride a bike and the pleasure
of independence and flight.

It was her neighbor from India who
showed her how to cook once a week
when you are single. How to take
a walk when you must celebrate
a holiday alone, how to trust
an invisible God when there is
no one to wake you up in the morning.

NIGHT BLOOMING

The honeysuckle blooms in pairs,
sets of four, the wick limbs
a pale green, the dead, perfect
kindling for lying by the bonfire
in the gentle rain.

NIGHT BLOOMING

Five Red Tears, or I am Not a Gardner

I planted sage but I had too much
so, I hung up wreathes to keep
away the dead.

I planted Holy Basil but it withered
and would not come back.

So I fed the birds and thousands
of thistle sprung up where
I didn't want them.

And when the goldfinch came,
I planted blue forget me nots,
but they pinked then waned to white
Today their centers are red.

Five red tears in each flower's face
Sometimes you want to be a gardener
but even the flowers cry.

Why do we think we have any say
about what grows?
Whatever will grow, will grow
with no say from you or I.

So I run away from my garden
Just for the day and go up town
to Broadway with the top down
in a stolen convertible
getting stuck in traffic is never
more glorious.

Men on motorcycles wink. Traffic
cops nod. The sun shines gold
off the steeple of Our Lady
of Perpetual help.

But the flowers have snuck in with me.
Back seat drivers, they call loudly in the wind

NIGHT BLOOMING

"Don't You need help?"
Ignoring them, I circle Midtown
then back across the river toward home,
when an empty strawberry container
blows across the mess of lanes rattling
across the highway in front of me
clear as a ghost.

The tribes who once protected this prairie
say that when a loved one dies, they walk
among the Strawberries.

There is so much loss in a basket
empty of strawberries
while some gardens are full new plants
spring among the herbs and profusion
of Penny Royal, but in other gardens
there are no strawberries. In other gardens,
there are no ghosts. In other gardens,
there are no ancestors to return to
because we haven't eyes to see them.

Maybe you are missing someone?
But aren't they still here?
Speaking to us from the ground ?
Sending us wind to dry our tears,
signs and wonders, blossoms of red
where we planted something else entirely?

What if we thank them for their stories,
their red blood in our veins, their beauty and bud
their bold moments of ripeness?

So, I have forgotten my blue for-get-me nots
to treasure what emerged –

Oh, and I returned
the car and planted more flowers–
harvested sage.

NIGHT BLOOMING

Poet-Trees

Behind my old apartment parted
in the trees, a small forest grew.
Wild turkey roamed
daily to feast on the neighbor's
spread for hard yellow corn.

With little money for meat,
starving, pregnant, I planned
a dozen wily ways to kill
and cook that turkey.

I'd drop a stone on the plumpest,
hit it with my car, use a box trap,
or buy a cap gun, and *bang*, dinner.

Instead, we moved, to a house,
I learned to write poetry
and eat words instead.

A decade later, my babies grown
the food bank, mostly history,
driving past, I see them.
There, stacked on the side of the road
chopped into logs like so many bundles.
My small forest, gone.

The death of trees—
Why are poets
always stricken
when trees are cut down?

Maybe we used to be trees
in another life? But once lost,
were born again into the world
as people, so that we could get another
chance to speak— about the wind, the
blossoms of seasons the red fan of fall,
of quickening of time, and the haste of death,
the shortness of love, the sturdiness of
good neighbors, how to lean into a storm.

NIGHT BLOOMING

As trees somehow, we
were not heard, so we trees rustle
and whisper, twist with time's tempests,
use words formed with letters rather
than rings of being, and then

we put them into books, books
made of leaves and they whisper
quietly, they whisper quietly.

NIGHT BLOOMING

Emily Dickinson is addicted to Facebook

The paper birch tree outside my door
Does he secretly hate me while I love him?
Did the ancients use his bark to bait their signs—
to page the memories bud come?

I leave him hanging loose
coiled in sheaves roiled in rolls
He has paper for me
but I've no words to write.
What I mean is, shuddering
there in shreds with not a stitch
would he rather be naked
and I a writer?

So I will tear one sheet off
here to enshrine and pray
the bitter cold won't wound him.
I can't tell what his nature
may be, but maybe this poet here
can tell. Emily Dickinson stands
by the window every day with me
these last few pandemic months.

She's been muttering about
the Civil War in her sleep.
I'd say it's her position—
choosing to lounge there
on the dog bed prone posed—
sometimes feet tapping against
the window, other times
asleep like a cat—

she refuses to leave the office—
I'd say surely, she and the tree share
a secret, if I didn't know already that
Emily Dickinson is addicted
to Facebook. Yes, Emily
Dickinson is addicted to Facebook—

She's up all night talking to poets
and posting on the daily

NIGHT BLOOMING

poetry page. Then again
in the mornings, she does seem to
have a daily conversation with my tree
outside the office window.

I'm worried she will steal
him away somehow take him
back to Massachusetts.
I mean if she can time travel,
she can do anything. If I could speak
to my tree, I'd tell him
my position is not to write
in words at all but in pictures for
they have words inside, more
than you might imagine.

I never say a word about 1864
and neither does Emily.
I crest each wave of nightly news,
get woke about what's civil,
speak less each day. But I owe her.
I'd be losing my mind
if it weren't for Emily here with me.
And she'd be losing her mind
if it weren't for her 1844
Webster's American dictionary.

She's always reading it aloud,
then laughing as though it had revealed
something scandalous or worthy
of meditation. I tried to tell her
that I'm related to Webster, but she
pretends she can't hear me.
She thinks I'm the ghost.
I say it's her, but the more
Covid19 stretches on,
I'm beginning to agree with her.

While I'm hitting month three
of isolation, and teaching myself to swear,
Emily just peers at her scanning,
sewing together rhythms that
will slap the unsuspecting reader

NIGHT BLOOMING

in the face to confound them.
—

While I type in the darkening room,
my wrist hurts like I'm digging
out of internment. She writes
on the scraps I leave lying about.

Emily thinks post-it notes are funny
and sometimes she puts them
on her forehead
and giggles at some game.

While she can study one word
for a whole day, a week, a year,
I would sell my iPad for just one word
that pulls its weight, or flies
– either one.

The only word I have now is *"bee."*
 Damn it all, Emily, I can't get your bee
out of my mind. Its voice–the delicate
newness of its wings makes it buzz
as loud as dictionaries being stroked
the wrong way.

Emily talks to trees like me
No, she is a tree too I think, a poet-tree.
Each poem, a leaf she stitches in time.
I'm not sure there's enough of me
To be one, but maybe if you added
me, one wordless poet
and added myself again–
or how much the same
four quarters of one person—
Let's say my two brothers
and my sister and me—
Wrap us together with bark
and we'd make one tree.
Hand us pen and paper
and we'd write a one-quarter column each,
our limbs held out writing on each other's backs
One in Braille, one in sound,
one runes, and me, in poetry —

NIGHT BLOOMING

Four years ago, I named the art gallery
"Paper Birch" after my own tree
so I'd remember to let the poets climb in
I wanted to hand out free post-its and declare
that keeping trees warm, well clothed,
and chaste was never the point of a writer.
Winter may be about whiteness
but it's the black soul underneath
poets want to dig.

The edge of our points were always swords
and walking sticks over matter.
So, no matter how much I love this tree,
really love him, I think ink
means more than paper, and maybe
that's what he's been trying to tell me,
dropping pages and shaking
his limbs in my face every morning.

And when she goes home, Emily—
will have to loan me her bee
because folios are better than cross stitch,
and oxygen–oxygen is overrated–
when I've always been a tree anyway.

When Emily goes home,
I'm giving her my iPad,
and she's letting me keep
her bee.

NIGHT BLOOMING

Turn, Turn Blackened Catfish

Over tea, the spoons rattle.
Her purse is pinched in her left hand,
Sassy shakes pepper over blackened
catfish, but she isn't looking
either of us in the eye.

On the table, the black-eyed peas
speak for her, their watery voices
rise from her plate,

*"What if we did something other than
simply to survive?"*

"Make sure to keep your receipt!"
he must have told her because
Sassy circles the date—folds
it neatly in her purse
with a compunctious smile.

Later she'll hand the receipt to him,
mention he had asked for it, he'll say,

"I never said that."

Adam might have said it first,
*"You can always return the fruit
later if you don't like it, but, Eve, keep the receipt."*

Sassy's sister says she's not really
allowed to be out with me.

*"You're wasting a whole hour
to have lunch with that
friend of yours,"* he'll say.
"You could be working."

He'll go get his haircut—to enjoy
a decollate and steamed towels.
Afterwards, he'll grab take out.
She skips lunch most days
to save money.

NIGHT BLOOMING

Every month, she cuts her hair
herself then dyes it over the sink.
The red color, a box from
a twenty-four-hour Walmart run.

Wearing pajamas at midnight,
in the toothpaste aisle, two men
squeeze past her on both sides
When had she become invisible?

Sassy keeps the leftover dye carefully
separated into two baby food jars.
She can make it last for a few more
treatments, her hair looks shiny
because she air dries to save conditioner.

Tomorrow, Sassy will drive in the rain
to an interview. The car will start
sliding all over the beltway–
two kids in the back.

At the service station,
she'll give the kids chocolate,
then the tire guy will quietly share his news
while eyeing the two
children with pity,

"I've never seen tires this bald.
You need four new ones.
Right now."

Sassy knows she doesn't have enough
for two tires, let alone four.
 She rummages in her purse for
an answer but there is no money,
only receipts
carefully ordered by date
so she can pass an inspection
at a moment's notice.

Something sizzles and snaps.
Sassy stands up,
Gives the tire man a hard stare,

NIGHT BLOOMING

sizes him up and down
for any signs of weakness.
Receipts begin to fly out of her purse
emerge from her hair and shoulders
falling off her like feathers,
her hair burns bright
the color of copy pennies.
Her eyes flash darkly,

like the black-eyed peas are
giving her new strength and stamina,
growing through her veins,
rooting her feet to the floor–their words
entering her blood stream–their
invisible leaves reaching up to clouds.

*"I have a hundred and
eighty-four dollars. You will
find me four tires,"*
she says evenly, *"I do not care
if they've just been taken off another car, if...
they are from the trash pile.
You will put them on my car, and
I will pay you what I have."*

Back home, alive, on four tires, no job, two
kids, zero in the bank.
Sassy sees, he's bought a new Wii.

"But it's used," he says, *"and
I'm doing a crossword–
How do you spell 'unconcerned?'
What are you going to cook
for dinner?"*

Sassy will probably make dinner.
She's not the leaving type.
Last week the chiropractor told her,

*"Most people, like you,
who are unresponsive to treatment
have been car crash victims
or have had serious falls.*

NIGHT BLOOMING

Do you remember falling recently?"
Sassy can't remember if she fell.
She's can't remember her middle name
anymore—or her birthday.
Was it Sara or November, Elizabeth
or something else?

She's pretty sure she hasn't fallen
but when she goes home and walks
through the gate into the
backyard she does remember falling
there, or was that a dream?

The next day, Sassy will go
to the doctor for memory loss.

"Keep a list of things you forget,
the doctor will tell her. *"Bring it back
with you, next time you come."*

"We should work out together more,"
he says to Sassy after she gets home
and puts the baby to bed.
She sits down
for the first time in eighteen hours.

He turns on his favorite movie again.
She sits next to him, sees fuzz
like the time she was little
and the twelve-inch TV—
black and white—had
only twelve channels
two that worked—
sometimes three or four.

She used to stand up from the ivory
Naugahyde couch, turn the knob
one channel to the right—

"Turn it back! No, the other way,"
her parents would say
until they got to *He-Haw*
and the banjo would play.

NIGHT BLOOMING

Then she'd sit between them
and they would both laugh, swirling
glasses of instant iced tea. It was
better than surviving.

"There is a season for everything," Sassy says
humming the tune
as she stands up and turns off the T.V.

She's just remembered her name.
Tonight, she's going to get up at
three a.m. and pack while he's asleep.
She'll leave the receipts.

Justice is Running

Take me to Kansas City
where Justice is running for office.
"Equality improves policy,"
he cries. Take me to 38th
where we'll skateboard
in yellow Nikes–cool as a cucumber,
cool as Prospero's basement book
on 39th, Take me to Kansas City
to a shirtwaist house, bed rock
on the bottom, blue collar on top.

Take me to the poet's house
 her garden lined with blue bottles,
where mint blossoms bend
under butterflies
and a broken wheelbarrow
boasts a fairy land
rosy bowling balls rest
under an old ash tree
while little suns
glint over her dark door
the poet's house–where justice runs.

Take me to Kansas City
where Justice is running
where in violence
by the numbers
we're always in the top ten.
Take me to Kansas City where
Justice is running, where
the red lines were drawn, and
the banks picked one side.

Take me to Kansas City
where Justice is running, where
artists move every six months,
but they never stop dancing
where restaurants spring up
and some people get to eat at them.
Where showboats take the poor
and the rich have every

NIGHT BLOOMING

thing they need.

Take me to Kansas City
to the poet's house, her door
open, her heart rolled out
to the Main Street
Her garden bed
covered in cast off crystals,
in opals and bottle caps, in oyster
shells and words. Justice is Running,
she writes to patch the roofs, and paint
the doors. Justice is running

changing the names
of the roads as she flies by.
Justice is running to serve tacos
under the bridge, to stop homelessness
from being illegal, to take bullets
from where they are lodged
in the air. Justice
sets up her tent in the street.
She and the poet try bowling
for tacos, bowling for salsa, bowling
for frijoles, bowling for love.
They share everything they make
with enough time left to sit on
a porch swing on 38th street,
with enough time left to carve
the bowling balls on a lathe
into hundreds of wheels,
to make skateboards for all
the neighboring kids,

so they too can fly, so they too
can go into the street,
and step gold, step gold
everywhere and set
their own justice down
on fragile wings
in a new garden of swings.

NIGHT BLOOMING

Evening Rock

Field Stones

When preparing a field
make fences out of the rocks
in the way.

NIGHT BLOOMING

unedited prayer garden

Our gardener who art in heaven
succulents sprout anew like
hens and chicks plump like the little
plaster angel holding a puppy
Hallowed is thy name
among the carnations
shells and corals
tulips and pink daffodil
thy kingdom come
thy will be done among
the snails and roly–polies
among the robins planning
up for spring
the paving stones that say
there's no place like home
on earth in earth and
around the mums
as it is in heavenly holy basil
give us this day our strawberries
and pansies as heavenly blue
as cherubs' wings like all that
is good and holy let peonies
bloom like clouds
with silver linings and forgive
the little ants and woodlice
forgive the bees, the spiders,
the pealing paper birch tree
forgive the dandelions who are
only stars
forgive us, lord,
with moss and rain, and
lead us not– lead us not back
to winter
deliver us from drought and scorch
from powers from root rot. For
yours is this garden and
yours is the garden—and yours
is the garden. amen

NIGHT BLOOMING

What you see here

What you see here is the aftermath
a burning star, the explosive
emptiness of what used to be
The table scrapes when we take
out the extra leaf to make it smaller
dinners are informal–
sometimes two or three–
constellations of conversations
emerge as partial images,
four or five gather on holidays,
and above the table, a chandelier
though no one can quite reach
the lights

I'm the reticent head of it, the table
when I remember not to sit
underneath–What you see here
is the aftermath, the dying out,
the halving of a small family,
growing smaller day by day. I used to
iron the napkins, polish the wood,
but now the table's painted blue
for the open space we set our sights
on, and for the sky outside glass
where I sit and watch birds
come to look for crumbs

It's a peaceful circle–maple
heavy, round enough
for cards, or breakfast with coffee,
here at the table, we solve problems
like what day the milk will be
delivered, and which idea will be
the next best thing.

The table wobbles under its hundred
years of servitude but I think it listens
to us as we do homework, pray, sing
over candles–Maybe the table thinks

NIGHT BLOOMING

I've been too harsh explaining what
life is like here—He says
it hasn't been too bad, quite wonderful
actually—except that we often forget to
keep him free of crumbs

What you see here is a family
small and true, in and out,
shrinking, then growing again,
dogs get fed treats under the table
and someone always scolds that
we shouldn't spoil them
The table is happy and has extra leaves
For when more people do come
and he says that is all that matters

Knock on wood

You try not to think about the dead

You try not to think about the dead
the same bread
from two such different trees
You want to live again
breathing for words,
Time over temperature.
Rise over run
Be your own father
What if love?
Feet in the grass
Bridges over stolen water
Soft rock to lean on
safely through winter–
Surely, you are not lost.
At night, you find the owl who laughs
hear whispers in the ground
from reticent moles who chat about
their "Joseph life." Like you,
they've spent fourteen years underground
with only dreams to eat.
The owl screeches it's the "Jacob life"
you've had more trouble with–
seven years of envy chasing
the small chance for a turn.
You'd trade this blanket of night
for enough breath to blow away
this silent carnival for
any dream at all––All you want is for
your feet to work, and your wings
to hold back a little longer
Just you watch out, Chrysalis
you're a butterfly no more.
Just you watch out, Chrysalis
whether tears or laughter
the old life will simply
get too small and bust open.
All or nothing, those wings,
your wings, will come.

NIGHT BLOOMING

The Aldica—

January 2020
I bought too much but didn't spend
much money-- canned soup
from Germany gluten free rice chips,
frozen salmon and ice cream
for my birthday—the kids like
mint chocolate chip.

Inside the sliding glass door a stout
mom with an infant strapped to her
middle, packs groceries into sacks.
Her toddler sits on the counter.

"*Stop playing and around
and help me,*" she says.

The security officer stares
into his phone, a boy just
out of basketball, bent to one side
as if each movement of his finger
were his last, like if he leans even
further he'd be back in school.
I push my cart out into the lot,
cars parked like long loaves of bread,
the wind whips my eyes closed
just as I see–

–*It's a full moon in the Aldi's Parking lot*
in the middle of January.
People rush in for a snowy weekend
and the Super Bowl but right now,
it's warm as cooled toast,
the windows are down, coats are off.
Traffic crawls by like beetles to a feast

–*It's a full moon in the Aldi's parking lot*
An airplane roams silently overhead,
the clouds sweep back like shopping
bags, the trees ignored like a list
of ingredients over a paper-box sky.

NIGHT BLOOMING

—It's a full moon in the Aldi's parking lot
A policeman, rosy cheeks, bald head
in his off-duty t-shirt, waves
to a friend, people go in and out
of the door with quarters
thinking half thoughts and full
thoughts about what life's about,
their musings like so many blueberries
shipped from Mexico. Their steps
like piles of vanilla wafers
around the spilled milk.

—It's a full moon in the Aldi's parking lot
and everyone is going home to dinner
the African man in the blue starched
shirt. The girl in short shorts
with a tiny purse hanging past
her hemline. People stuffing trunks
full as olives while kids with grapey
smiles ride on the backs of carts.
Mothers, hair in messy buns,
glasses as round as eggs push
them like loads of future happy meals,
loads of laundry, loads of pop.

People look at me in the eye
they smile at me as I walk very
slowly to my car, people
who could have been
in my fourth grade class
who could have been my banker,
my teacher, my nurse, but now
we are all just happy
and smiling from the warmth
under the paper plate moon,
under a blue salt sky.

—It's a full moon in the Aldi's parking lot
and someone hands me a sweaty quarter
as they take my cart out of my hands
A tired tiny woman with red cheeks
leaves her cart up front
and walks to her car like a bird after a storm.

NIGHT BLOOMING

June 4, 2020
Leave my glasses in the car
so my mask won't steam them up
It means I can't read,
but I have Aldi's memorized.
My son wears a green plaid mask,
I have blue polka dots. The store
almost empty
just two ladies laughing,
everyone is ordering online now.

I rush because
some of the shelves are empty.
Signs say, "limit two."
Fear means I buy random things–
like iced chocolate bananas.
No sweet potatoes,
so we take frozen fries.
No baking soda, no ginger.
No eggplant, tomatoes.

We haven't left the house in weeks.
We go wild with sauces, organic
gummy bears. Two bags of greens,
Missouri seedless watermelon.
The check out lady, invisible
behind a plastic shield and mask.

My clothes need mended
but who will care here?
My son is homeschooled now,
he helps bag the cold food. I do
the rest, but smush the bread.

The security guard wears all brown,
comes late from a break.
Probably young,
but he looks middle aged with
a donut belly and haircut
like a young friar tuck.
In the parking lot, black capped
chickadees sing in pairs
to a sunset as pink as lemonade.

NIGHT BLOOMING

The clouds are low like paper dragons
the moon waxing full, a porcelain plate.

January 2021
I brought my own quarter today
asked my twelve-year-old to help me.
We have a pattern.
He waits for me to fix my hair and mask,
get my purse, then
he carries the quarter.
An offering. We bring bags this time.
And extra to leave behind.
I get some of everything because
who knows what food will be here
tomorrow. I buy junk food
for the long monotonous weeks.
Cheese curls. Oreos. Pringles.
Chicken, organic fruit and veg.
On a bench an old man, dark skin,
grey hair, sits like Mr. Rogers
in a dapper hat, elbow patches,
legs crossed.

The checkout guy looks
as young as my son
behind his plexiglass. We box and bag
like for like. Cold and hot.
Veg and fruit. Bread and eggs.
We have a system. We lift heavy
bags together without counting.
We pack the cart and walk out
the sliding glass door.

The Security guard like wax,
arms crossed. Once the trunk
is filled, eggs and bread on top,
my son takes the cart back, he knows
to leave the quarter.

In the parking lot,
a mom pushes a little girl in her cart,
a girl with perfect pom poms in her hair
she waves to me from their old Cadillac,

NIGHT BLOOMING

I wave too. Though in masks,
neither of us know if we smile.

Fall 2021
The doorbell rings- bags
mysteriously appear. Paper bags
filled to the middle. Folded over
stapled just so. A box of canned goods.
We accidentally ordered double
cucumbers, double celery.
We put them away easily
and fold the bags for recycling.
Canned tuna. Chocolate cereal.
Later the bell rings again. The driver
a short medium skinned woman
with shoulder length straightened hair
and a red coat brings us a bag of apples.
She had forgotten to give them to us,
they had fallen out. Wherever she drove
back from, her long day on wheels.
Dear Lord, Bless this Aldi's angel.

October 2021
Aldi's has a facelift. The poor
and crippled, aren't here anymore,
rich people come, confused
never having seen a quarter.
The sign says "next time online"
a girl with an owl covered blanket
rides in her mother's cart.
Everything is hit or miss. Gone or full.
The checker absently smashes our food,
patiently asks my son to
"put the cart back to the side"
so she can use it for the next person.
She washes it off first maybe, I'm not sure.

We bag, hardly speaking,
holding out things,
assigning cold food or bread
to each bag. Cans in a box.
Veggies and fruit. Dairy.
Who cares what we eat

NIGHT BLOOMING

Every day is the same.
Some Thursdays we
Go to the food line,
some Wednesdays
to the school for free food.
There's no security guard.
The day started out warm
but now cold and grey.

January 2022
"Your groceries are here,"
the text reads
"Review your tip for Angela."
I go outside but Angela from Aldi's
is already gone.
Three bags of warming groceries
sit by the welcome mat which used to
read, "living the dream"
but now just reads "dream."

Jerusalem Café is gone

Jerusalem Cafe is gone
the stones painted over.
A Formica table filled with
chicken and waffles. I

remember Jerusalem
sitting in the pizza shop
with the 500-year-old
brick oven, cats running

wild in the paved arch
laden streets. Old places
lay down and new ones
cross over, resting in

layers of story upon story.
All I want is a hot meal
and someone to tell me
how old the stones are.

here. Surely all stones are
from an age before men.
They know the things we do
not. Our life is short, they

believe our fires small
compared to their deep ruptures.
Stones trust in the future
they know that someday
their voices will return.

Garages

Old river stone are the
foundations in our city
grandfathered
garages made of lode
stones from a lost
ocean, long since
gone. So we build
garages with rocks
cut from the sea floor,
layers of crust, and we
add a door.
Then we bury things in
there. What we do carry to
the cellar but things we
want to forget about,
things we want to
remember, things we wish
were at the bottom of an
ocean now dry, things we
want to hold on to but
should have long since let
go, like the sea knowing
we've always been Atlantis
we've always been rising
only to sink again.

Easter Again 2021

It's 2:30 am Easter 2021 so I start another
poem. Number twenty-one give or take a few.

That first easter poem I wrote when I had no
money for candy to put in a basket. I knew
words were free, but once a year became
dozens became hundreds. Words are dangerous.

Poetry is dangerous.
When we take a Word and
give it a coat, tell it to take a place at the
table–set out grandma's linen napkins
embroidered with a "D"
for her step father's name–
When we tell the Word to take
a seat, and place our best silver from
under the cupboard, the porcelain
from Japan, we set a place for Elijah

In a poem Elijah can come back
to earth on his fiery chariot
to eat with us. I'll find something
kosher in the fridge and some olives to eat.
When we settle in with a cup of our best
coffee, we'll tell him about the first church
service we've been in a year. Outside in the
sunlight. How it feels to see a human face
again, after so much time alone indoors.

I'll ask him why he came to Easter dinner,
he'll say to tell us that miracles still exist.
Someone will probably argue and ask, How
he can even say that?

"Because God still exists," he'll say. *"We
have coffee every morning–almost
as good as this cup."*

"Has your oil ever run out?" he'll ask.
"What about your flour?"

NIGHT BLOOMING

At each question we will have to say,
"No, Elijah. You're right.
*Every year flowers grow. That one time
we didn't have food, the food
bank did, the church did, our neighbor's
brought us eggs and oranges. The check
finally came, right on time. No, what we truly
needed has never run out. No, when we
needed a friend or a family someone was
always there. Maybe not who we expected.
But someone. And when no-one was there.
God was. We did feel him. We felt him there."*

Then we'll hang our heads and remember
so many times, we didn't have one crumb of
faith. Elijah will remind us, God sent birds to
feed us, while I placed toy bunnies and birds
in baskets, a candy filled toy alligator, even
a shark or two.

Maybe Easter is a good time–a good
time to laugh at danger like the golden
egg I drop deep into the
well of an old stump for the egg hunt
because at least one child will risk the dark
in hope of treasure.

The children, now
too old for dresses and suits,
will wear flannel and jeans
on this cold rainy day.
They will run around
find the eggs anyway,
dumping out candy and quarters
with barks of laughter.

I'll bake a cake in the shape of a lamb,
and everyone will laugh at my attempt,
while the lamb who was worthy
Jesus surely must be here
in the kitchen, invisible,
as we pray over our meal.
Invisible, while the kids

NIGHT BLOOMING

search for treasures.
Course he's seen if you look for him—
He's our sacrifice, he's closing the gap,
making a way for us to travel that
long dark travail
to reach real Kingdom light
A place where things never run out.
Where loneliness
hasn't even been invented
where tears aren't needed anymore.

And after dinner, Uncle Joe
will play his violin
from Bach to fiddle. The music
will say that maybe life
is full of broken glass, smoke alarms,
and wild things but God
can use anything for good,
and God is setting a table for us.
He'll put out plates and the linens.
And he's waiting for us.

He's waiting for us to
see him face to face.

Stones

If you open this rock
inside its dark heart
you will find stars
 and inside those
  stars you will
   find stones

NIGHT BLOOMING

Sometimes You Finally get a Moment

sometimes you finally get a moment
sneak out the back gate after
watering your garden late–
consisting of one tomato and one

carrot step gingerly over snake holes
feet sinking into the tops of mole hills
pause over orchid like blossoms
from a tree you've never noticed before

cross the gambling spring
but you don't stop to gaze
your fingers skim the railings of
the rough cedar bridge–

a meandering path in a darkening
wood–passing empty benches cause
all the walkers have gone home
for the day

sometimes you finally get a moment
but the honeysuckle is unlistening
the gooseberries picked over–
young birds already fledged and flying

sometimes you finally get a moment
but things have changed
a different name carved into the log
you once knew as tree

sure, the path stops short
the dragonflies colorless or black
even the wild roses are naked--stubs
the cicadas count down for the day

but here the sidewalk ends you'll
have to decide
if you'll keep on the dirt path
or if you'll turn around and go home
then again sometimes you finally

NIGHT BLOOMING

get a moment —so you stop to write
a poem instead and that's when
the sky will come up to meet you

fingers flush and bloom
a shade of pink over green
you've never seen before—
that's when you know

it's not too late perhaps—
petals or sunbeams, saplings
or stumps, your heart is young
and that will make all the difference

NIGHT BLOOMING

Night Blooming

Fattening Moon

Here rises the fattening moon
made of licorice and the absence
of night as I walk over a roiling hill
past hellhounds quieting
the cicadas slumber in the cold
only my wide footsteps on the
road under this cosmic mirror
prove my dream is to wait for words
words to lessen this incline
to fill up this plain

NIGHT BLOOMING

Skyscrapers

It's night here.
My mother dances a doll's dress
crocheted with sky-colored yarn
into a Ginger Rodgers two-step,
bursts into song,

and for the first time,
I know I'm not the only one—
a Pollyanna,
a-shooting-star-idealist-
pie-in-the-sky-over-rainbows
kind of girl.

But what will happen
to my own kids raised by us, two
skyscrapers who've trouble backing down
from the heights of our ideals
who can't raise our voice in anger?

Skyscrapers can't reach
the height of intentions
to mirror our grand plans
Stories upon stories they rise
just to reach the hem
of our first step.
After all, skyscrapers
are only empty spaces
where the sky should be-
voids of what we might see
Turn them upside down
and they are roots
aimed at the heart of the earth
where my own progeny
born like from Athena's lighting,
or a basket of feathers
left by a seabird-two seeds
in an uncanny world.
without smell or taste,
a world of numbers, a world

NIGHT BLOOMING

where they picture "happy"
as white letters on a black ground
while I see it as a pink balloon.

The skyscrapers too are white
on a black ground–
lit in the darkening sky.
The skyscrapers are empty
and their lights dark
so maybe down here on the ground,
it's time to return to singing.
I never told anyone
that it was a photograph
in a dream of my great-
grandparents just back from
fishing that made me come
home to Kansas City.

Funny the photo was cropped
badly, their heads cut off
above the shoulders,
their hips lost below the waist
even the fish were cropped
out of the picture,
but I still knew it was them by the
fabric of their intentions
and I knew– I needed
to come home
to these muddy stolen waters.
Let's get a boat and go fishing
just you and me.
I'll cast line after line
searching for a treasure.
What do I have to leave
for my two-taled kids
except these lines. in hope
they will go to the water and listen,
tell a good story,
flip the world
any direction they please,
that whenever they stand up,
they'll have the sudden urge to fly.

Night Blooming Flower

A late night knock on our door.
It was back in that little town near the
Susquehanna? That one where beautiful
poppies grew in front of white porches
where wreaths change on doors by season
and the old water mill still stands by the creek.

It's time.

I gather up the baby, put her on my hip—
no shoes. Quickly, we wander over
the steppingstone yard past crocus
and the mud smell of the nearby pond
The sky—orange and purple mixed
together.

Sue and Bob meet us at the mailbox
under their budding maple
heavy with seeds, across one lumpy lawn
through the dwelling dark. With hushed

murmurs, we step over roots and leaves
cracks in the sidewalk our expectant joy like
a river growing from winter runoff.
We enter the small white sun porch, cerulean
in the darkening night. The old screen door

slams and scuttles as we each bump
inside—one, two, three, four, five
of us join the others jammed around the wicker
chairs and table, though none of us sit.

We mesh together legs and arms, neighbors
in sweaters and house slippers holding on
to each other—fingers lightly on shoulders
and hips so we don't crush
into the wonder.

There in the center
a shrub in a heavy ceramic pot
its trunk the size of a broom handle, leaves like

NIGHT BLOOMING

hands dark as ripe olives
sleek as magnolia leaves, and the proud mother
beside. Her smooth white hair like the buds
on the slowly opening flowers awakening
to the moonlight. Our bated breath like
small stars of warmth—we watch as the

blooms unfurl strong as teacups, open to the rising
moon their crepe paper petals so sure of themselves.

It only blooms once
in a lifetime and only
at night during a full moon.

Oh, to be a night–blooming flower to know that
for once in my long life, I would be beautiful,
I would be loved, and I would not
be afraid of the dark.

If I could go back in time, I'd take those flowers
to the cobbler and ask him to make a pair of shoes.
I'd put them on the baby
and teach her to walk like a person who knows

her worth— knows that the world is not made
of poppies but of light we can reflect
from the small of our backs, and the
force of a firm mind.

NIGHT BLOOMING

The Green Lady

Jazz trio at The Green Lady
down in Kansas City–
Jazz plays like a dream
down in Kansas City–
Quiet man on base
in a purple suit–
Poet man on base
in a mean suit.
White cap on brass–
Sweet, sweet brass.
Keyboard man in shades
in a dark room.
Lights like honeycomb
hang in a dark room.
Bar lit red waist down
bottles on the high wall–
Candlelight dusts up
gold painted tin tiles–
Hung like night sky
candlelit walls flicker.
Tiny round tables
lily pads in the moonlit.
Little island lights
warm on the inside
cold at night
warm on the inside–
That's one cold night!

NIGHT BLOOMING

Like Lightning

The clouds are rolling
the sky is full of dice
and she doesn't know what
a kind heart is like

Like a dog
in a thunderstorm
her heart hides away
unwilling to use the lightning
to find her next sure step

The clouds are rolling
the sky is full of dice
and she doesn't know what
a true heart is like

She is a comet
flinging through space
her veil, cold water,
and as she comes
around again she'll
look down
at the earth
and wonder what
it would be
like to
be

h
e
l
d

Moon White Dress

Why do we love the moon
her light cool as mushrooms
her valleys, the mark of battles won?
Aren't her changes but a stolen shadow,
her light merely borrowed?
The mirror of her coldness an echo
to a lost dare she never reasoned out.
Beginning a dance, with a stone in her shoe
to a song with apparently no end, or a friend
—at least anytime soon.

Has the moon ever been asked
what she wanted? Has the moon
always said yes, to the dress
laid out for her? Each night
black, or white. Each day

does she sleep and dream
of rainbows and plaids
bows and ribbons, contemplate
what air might be?
If she could only breathe?

Has she secretly wondered
what would happen if she
had an inner fire to kindle?
A light to bloom within,
or only a match?

NIGHT BLOOMING

"it's a terrible, terrible world."

"It's a terrible, terrible world"
she said every time,
before hanging up the phone,
before hugging me goodbye.
No not the wicked witch of the west,

Grandma Alice
from the gray plains of Kansas.
Her half-sister was Dorothy the one
that flew off with boys, that
turned back the grandfather clock
to keep her broken curfew hid.

"It's a terrible, terrible world"
she'd shudder
actual shivering

"It's a terrible, terrible world"
   -Okay, Grandma
"It's a terrible, terrible world"
   -I don't think so, Grandma
"It's a terrible, terrible world"
   -Grandma, it's not that bad,
But no reply I ever made in the
thirty-five years
we shared this earth together
ever made a difference.

Thousands of times
I looked for a comeback.
But like spools in her
abandoned sewing box,
each thread my promise
I'd prove her wrong.

I looked under burnt houses,
at the back end of broom sticks
car wrecks, and missed baby carriages
in graveyards, but
nowhere did a good world appear.

NIGHT BLOOMING

"It's a terrible, terrible world,"
she shivered
—actual shuddering
her throat—would catch.

"It's a terrible, terrible world"
    -But we'll make it better, Grandma
"It's a terrible, terrible world"
    -Grandma, we are trying
"It's a terrible, terrible world"
    -Not all the time
But nothing could convince her.

Wars later, a plague or two
some recessions, and depressions,
I'm wondering about that woman
who grew up in the twenties because
her mini-me is too. Grand baby
has the same curl over forehead,
same dimple in her left elbow,
when she stands with one
hand on one hip, I shiver, uncanny
as she tells me
how bad the world is-

Much worse than 100 years ago,
much worse than in Dickens time,
much worse than during monarchies,
much worse than old wars,
much worse.

And I say,

    -we are trying.
    -it's not all bad.
    -we are working on that
    -Some things are better
But she doesn't believe me.

When I dream, my grandmother
has the blue face of a goddess palm down.
My grandfather is a chieftain.
Each try to prove their story is right,

NIGHT BLOOMING

each want an offering I cannot bring.

"It's a terrible, terrible world,"
she would shudder, goosebumps
going up her arms, the hair on her
neck would stand on end.

And now, just when I think
she might be right, I see it.
It wasn't a curse, but a blessing.
like "break a leg" before the Scottish play.
It was her way of hoping, a prayer
that I would be spared
the worst pain.

"It's a terrible, terrible world,"
she'd say before hanging up the phone.
  -I love you too, I answer

It's the twenties again.
I don't have many rights, or money.
I don't have much health care.
I'm an indentured servant
to my college loans.
I just quit my job earning
half of minimum wage. There's
no where I can pray
on a Sunday, but I'm
safe for now. Today there's food
in the pantry and I've prepared
for the worst.

Yes, it's a "terrible, terrible world,"
I tell you, but I'm a poet
and a word can mean what
I say it means. Terrible imperfection
terrible humanness, terrible love
and where these closed doors,
these broken scales try to beat me,
I'll turn around and
face the open prairie. I'll mix sun
in my rain with a teaspoon
and I'll find that good world

NIGHT BLOOMING

yet. And it will be terrible
it will be fierce and I'll
pound it into a path
made of poems, for us
to walk across.

NIGHT BLOOMING

night garden cantos

i. frogs first

the frogs are singing for the first
evening of spring—the blue edges of sky
fold closed echoing their tiny peeps—
only in a poem, can you get a peep
out of me—some poets ask which me
came first the tree or the mushroom,
the poem or the poet-tree
which side will make us taller,
which side makes us free?
the frogs tell me
—sing
—sing
—sing
sing in the night garden.

Penny tells me, *everything is about joy*
Patience says,
everything is about suffering
i'd like to put those two together
—two tracks
and i'll ride my train down those rails
with each rickety bump
another iron neglected will hold

what is the name of the thing
that holds us together
—vine?
—peg?
—string?
if only words could wrap around us

what if we could be in Neruda's Ocean where
what if unity is where we swim--where water is us
where we bloom arms and fingers
like wise salamanders
and for the first time what if we knew
that we are writers
like him, we'll write an ode to an onion
cry, then write it again

NIGHT BLOOMING

ii. *next door*

what if everything about
this year was about our neighbors
if we could hop over the fence and say
"we're sorry"
i'll give them a basket of eggs
i'll train my dog not to attack
not to protect me
when I'm afraid because
I'm afraid of everything–
if i could retrain
my heart to sing like a bird
and my mouth to
whistle, it would be here
in the night garden

what is the sound of a blue jay
that makes my heart happy?
why can I walk on its darts
through the bold blue sky
and find poems hanging there
among the leaves?

Poet tells me that *life is poetry*
that it's the air we breathe, but I'd like
to find out what *is*...

iii. *it's night*

i'm digging for poems in my garden
because i've looked everywhere else.
you can come with me and dig too
Purpose tells us what *is* what *was* what *will be*,
who she *is*, who she *was*, and who she *will be*

sometimes we tell our students
"*is*" is the
weakest verb
–but is it?

NIGHT BLOOMING

because what will be is maybe
who we are--is maybe
who we could be
isn't half a poem what *is*
—a simile—like or as?

i'm digging in my garden for the is-ses
and was-es and will-be's,
and i'm pulling up weeds
of silence, weeds of doubt
words that never worked out
and if only i dig deep enough
i could find a poem
to sing to you

iv. *some of our brothers is*

some of our brothers have been locked up
for two years, two months, and two days,
and some of our brothers are never coming home

how will we remember them
sometimes i think that *is* is the strongest verb
because of what I need to be
i need to be strong

sometimes i think that *is* is the strongest verb
because of what i want to be
i want to be a poet but
the poet needs to be weak

what if we lash all the words together
if we ride a ship of dandelion fluff for sails
if we fly so high we breathe starlight?
you should know what happens
if you take dandelions to outer space?
—a thousand suns of yellow.

i tell my students sometimes
we tell our students sometimes
that "*is*"
is the weakest verb but is it?
a poet is

NIGHT BLOOMING

– a blue jay
–a peeper
–a flower
– a star

we are the whole night garden
glowing and growing and declaring

it is

NIGHT BLOOMING

Gems

You think poets arrange words
like a nosegay of flowers, stalks in hand.
You peer in my palm, hoping to find a gem.
But I tell you—Look deep. There, in the lifeline.
You see that sand? Poems are what is left over
when I stop to open my clenched fist and laugh.

Sometimes I write poetry
by waiting for gems to emerge.
I dig them out of the dirt.
brush them off set them aside
and hope for a complete set.
Other times they fall from the
sky like comets and there,
with a blazing tail I wonder
that they came to me.

ABOUT THE AUTHOR

POLLY ALICE MCCANN poet, artist, dreamer began writing poetry after a cold winter night in the desert with only a book for her pillow. She earned her BA in Studio Art. After her MFA in Writing from Hamline University in St. Paul, her poetry was published internationally in journals like *365 Days*, *Naugatuck River*, and *arc24* in Tel Aviv and elsewhere. Polly's art has been published in US newspapers and magazines most recently in Rattle magazine. An adjunct writing professor and creative consultant at pollymccann.com, she is also the founder and manager of FLYING KETCHUP PRESS. She credits much of her creative work due to her research on dreams and the subconscious writing process which won her the 2014 Ernest Hartmann award from Berkeley, CA. She loves to grow basil, teach, paint, and explore unexpected surprises with her kids and their short-eared hound dog.

Poetry Prompt with Polly

Lyrical Dickinson Prompt

Round 1: Read two Emily Dickinson poems and notice the beginning and end sounds of words. *Alliteration* is the repeated initial consonant or beginning sounds. *Assonance* is the repeated vowel sounds in multiple words. *Consonance* is any repeated consonant sounds in multiple words. Set that aside.
Next: Write for six minutes without stopping. Write in prose or poetry as many emotions a recent experience as possible.
Exception: You have to write about something very, very small; possibly insignificant to most people.
Extra: Choose one old fashioned emotional verb (swoon, harp etc.)and try and incorporate into the poem.

Round 2. Reread two Emily Dickinson poems. Set them aside.
Next: Turn your free write up a notch by editing your work to create as many intentional alliterations, assonance and consonance sounds as you feel comfortable.

Round 3. Optional rewrite the poem from that small object insignificant creature. Be spare as possible and disregard all thoughts to form or punctuation.

NIGHT BLOOMING

LOOK OUT FOR MORE POETRY BOOKS BY
Polly Alice McCann

Kinlight: Homegrown Poems, 2017
Tea with Alice: Heirloom Poems, 2019
Puss 'N Boötes: Dark Poems, 2020

Anthologies:
Blue City Poets: Kansas City 2019
The Very Edge: Poems 2020

FLYING KETCHUP PRESS to discover and develop new and diverse voices in poetry, drama, fiction and non–fiction with a special emphasis in new short stories. We are a publisher made by and for creatives with the spirit of the Heartland. Our dream is to salvage lost treasure troves of written and illustrated work– to create worlds of wonder and delight; to share stories. Maybe yours. Find us at www.flyingketchuppress.com.

www.ingramcontent.com/pod-product-compliance
Lightning Source LLC
Chambersburg PA
CBHW031459040426
42444CB00007B/1149